This book is dedicated to all who find Nature not an adversary to conquer and destroy, but a storehouse of infinite knowledge and experience linking man to all things past and present. They know conserving the natural environment is essential to our future well-being.

BLUE RIDGE PARKWAY

THE STORY BEHIND THE SCENERY®

by Margaret Rose Rives

Peggy Rives is a career employee of the National Park Service. After receiving her master's degree from the University of California at Los Angeles, she moved to the Blue Ridge Mountains of North Carolina. Here she developed an abiding love for these mountains and deep respect for the native mountain people, their heritage, and their way of life.

Blue Ridge Parkway, located in southern Virginia and northern North Carolina, was established in 1936 to protect the 469-mile-long parkway, natural history areas, and Appalachian cultural sites.

Front cover: Blue Ridge Parkway, photo by David Muench. Inside front cover: At the Peaks of Otter, photo by Walter McQuarry. Page 1: Flame azalea, photo by Glenn Van Nimwegen. Pages 2/3: Along the Parkway, photo by John Vavruska.

Edited by Mary L. Van Camp. Book design by K. C. DenDooven.

Sixth Printing, 2004
BLUE RIDGE PARKWAY: THE STORY BEHIND THE SCENERY © 1982 KC PUBLICATIONS, INC.
"The Story Behind the Scenery"; the Eagle / Flag icon on Front Cover are registered in the U.S. Patent and Trademark Office.
LC 82-82578. ISBN 0-916122-81-6

*T*here is a quality in mountains which touches our finer nature. Highland forests immerse us in the eternal rhythm of the natural world; immense unbounded vistas cause our spirits to expand. Riding the ridges of the southern Appalachians, the human soul soars freely.

High in the mountains of southern Appalachia there is a road to fulfill the motorist's dream: the Blue Ridge Parkway. For 469 miles it winds its graceful way like the melodious theme of a symphony, moving through quiet interludes of peaceful meadowlands and magnificent forests, increasing tempo as it climbs the ridges, and bursting into a glorious crescendo as it soars among the mountaintops. It is a highway designed for pleasure; it invites one to drive awhile, then stop awhile. Those who enjoy it to the fullest are in no particular hurry. There are overlooks opening on distant vistas of azure-hued mountains. Woodland paths invite one to walk in a shadowy green forest, or to pause beside a meandering mountain stream.

Time takes on a special quality on the Blue Ridge. After a few hours of driving on this magnificent road, one begins to forget the hurried pace, and the pressures of modern living. Visitors are soothed by the movement of shadows on the slopes below, the sighing of the wind in the trees, the songs of birds in the branches. In this longest national park, there is time to find a measure of peace. It is a place of changing seasons: of delicate fragrant blossoms in spring, warm golden days in summer, vibrant flaming color in fall, and crystalline snowy whiteness in winter. The scenic grandeur of the southern Appalachians is indeed worthy of a national park.

The Blue Ridge Parkway is more than a road, more than a monument to the incredible natural beauty of this region. Here in the mountains of southern Appalachia is the home of the southern highlander. The history and culture of these mountain people make this park different from the pristine wilderness areas of America's other national parks. In a sense, the Parkway is the people, who form a continuing living history of the mountain ways of life.

Mountains, forests, meadows, and mountain culture—these are the resources of the Blue Ridge Parkway. Visitors to the park will praise the virtues of their particular favorite, but on one topic all will agree. In the mountains of southern Appalachia lies one of the most beautiful highways in the world.

DAVID MUENCH

The Appalachian Mountains of the eastern United States extend from Maine to Georgia. Composed of many separate ranges, these mountains are among the oldest in the world. The rocks forming them vary from igneous to sedimentary and metamorphic, with many formations dating back to the Precambrian era. They tell a story of alter-

Ranges and Ridges

nating periods of deposition, upheaval, and erosion over hundreds of millions of years.

In the southern portion of the Appalachian system rises the Blue Ridge, a mountain chain extending from Pennsylvania to Georgia. Time has softened the aspect of these mountains—they seem gentle and friendly. Compared to younger mountains, they are not tall. Their highest peaks reach elevations of around 6,000 feet. However, "a mountain is impressive in proportion to its rise above the base." These mountains are steep, with many summits towering 4,000 feet above their valleys. It is also characteristic that in most places they are not orderly. They comprise a labyrinth of

On a spring evening after the rain, a delicate freshness pervades the atmosphere of the woods. Moisture enlivens the grasses and revitalizes the lichens growing on the trunks of oak trees.

steep inclines plunging into deep hollows, and sharp ridges rising abruptly from narrow, serpentine stream beds. Thus, while from a distance the southern Appalachians appear soft and rounded, they are quite rugged at closer view.

The ranges and ridges of Appalachia are covered by a luxuriance of plant life equaled in few other areas of the world. There are plants similar to those of China and Japan, part of the forest which once encircled the northern hemisphere. On the crests are trees of the Canadian forest; and in unequaled splendor on the slopes are the broadleafed trees—the eastern deciduous forest. This great diversity of vegetation is a gift from the Ice Age. On the southern edge of the ice sheet the ancient trees survived. When ice retreated, the northern trees followed to northern latitudes. But some species remained on the cool summits of the southern Appalachians: the northern conifers—spruces and firs; and the northern hardwoods—birches, maples, beeches, and red oaks.

The broadleafed trees evolved deciduous habits to preserve themselves by shedding their leaves in fall and sprouting new ones in spring. Although there are broadleafed trees in other parts of the world, the most extensive of these deciduous forests is to be found on the slopes of the Appalachian Mountains. In this forest there are 20 to 25 species of trees which are common; another 25 species are less common but are represented.

In the mixed forest there are Appalachian conifers: eastern hemlock, Carolina hemlock, white pine, and cedar. These mingle with southern hardwoods: oaks, locust, poplar, hickory, and cherry. Here once reigned the prolific American chestnut, beloved by early settlers for its durable wood and abundant nut crop. These magnificent trees were destroyed by a blight in the early part of the twentieth century—a sad reminder that nature's gifts are not impervious to destruction. Sprouts still come up from the old root stock and may reach a height of six or seven feet before they, too, succumb. Perhaps in time the chestnut will develop a resistance to the blight, and this once abundant tree will flourish again as part of the southern forest.

Its ancient ritual ever renewed, spring returns to the mountains. New leaves of delicate green emerge as the deciduous trees reclothe themselves. In joyful reaffirmation of life, tulip poplars reach for the sky.

DAVID CATLIN

With silent strength ferns push up through the forest floor, gracefully unfurling their fronds.

DAVID MUENCH

Rhododendrons of the southern Appalachians grow in dense entanglements of branches with evergreen leaves. Flower displays occur in June and July.

Beneath the deciduous trees of the southern Appalachians exists an incredible profusion of lesser vegetation: shrubs, vines, wildflowers, lichens, ferns, ground pines, mosses, and mushrooms. The rhododendron in places reaches tree proportions and grows in such a confusion of trunks and branches as to be impassable.

Beautiful at all times, the southern mountains are spectacular in spring and fall. The woods are full of flowers. First the wildflowers push their way up through last year's leaves. Then the flowering shrubs burst forth—purple and white rhododendron, delicate mountain laurel, and the blazing flame azalea. Overhead showy blossoms appear on many trees including locust, buckeye, black cherry, tulip poplar, and mountain magnolia. The succession of flowering lasts into the summer, and one has barely recovered from this beauty when fall arrives. The mountains become an artist's palette of brilliant color—reds, golds, greens, and yellows are liberally splashed upon the slopes. The eastern forests are surely one of nature's glories.

When the first settlers came to these mountains, they saw the greatest deciduous forest that had ever existed. It is hard for us to imagine what it must have been like when no saw blade had yet touched it. Remnants of the original forest remain: small stands in the Pisgah National Forest, in the Joyce Kilmer Memorial Forest, and in a few remote coves in the Great Smoky Mountains and the Blue Ridge.

Suggested Reading

BAKE, WILLIAM A. *Mountains and Meadowlands Along the Blue Ridge Parkway.* Washington, D.C. : U.S. National Park Service, Department of the Interior, 1975.

BROOKS, MAURICE. *The Appalachians.* Boston: Houghton Mifflin Co., 1965.

The constantly changing elevation of the Parkway allows for a prolonged bloom succession. A flowering species which has previously bloomed at a lower elevation may be reencountered on the heights a few weeks later.

DAVID MUENCH

Flowers of the fields and roadsides are resplendent with brilliant color throughout the summer months.

DAVID MUENCH

Settlement of the Blue Ridge

Although the high Appalachian Mountains were never heavily populated by Indians, evidence has been found of prehistoric occupation dating back 10,000 years. In the decades before the arrival of the white man, the mountains were used by Indians as hunting grounds and travel routes. The most powerful tribe, the Cherokee, had their center of habitation in the foothills of north Georgia and the mountains of eastern Tennessee. They also had smaller settlements throughout the mountains. East of the Blue Ridge dwelt the Catawba Indians; to the north were the Iroquois, Delaware, and Shawnee. The tribes fought over the great valley west of the Blue Ridge. Just before the coming of European settlers, the Iroquois had pushed the Cherokee and Catawba southward from the Shenandoah Valley.

Throughout the Blue Ridge were Indian trails for hunting, trading, and war. In the northern portion of the mountains the war party trace, or path, followed the high ridges; the peace trail followed the great valley. Their main trail forked at Big Lick, present site of Roanoke, Virginia. One route continued southwestward along the great valley and into the homeland of the Cherokee along the tributaries of the Tennessee River; the other route cut east across the Blue Ridge through the Roanoke River gap, then south into Catawba country. These Indian trails throughout the mountains usually followed buffalo trails. When the pioneers came, these were the paths they followed.

For settlements on the eastern seaboard, the mountains stood as a barrier to expansion for a century and a half. There were a few early explorers; the Spanish conquistador Hernando DeSoto ventured across the southern end of the Blue Ridge in 1540 seeking gold. He passed on through the wilderness to the Mississippi River. There were probably a few early hunters who ventured into the mountains, but the first recorded exploration of the Shenandoah Valley was made by John Lederer in 1669.

Around 1730 the first colonists began drifting into the mountains. Some descended the great valley from Pennsylvania; others followed Indian trails and river valleys westward from coastal settlements in the Carolinas. By the time of the Indian wars in the 1750s, western Virginia was thinly settled, but the mountains of western North Carolina remained a hostile wilderness. When Daniel Boone explored these mountains on hunting trips in 1760, there were few settlers. There were scattered communities by 1770, but the

BILL BAKE

In the old days, a work horse eased the load of plowing by hand. Today in Appalachia there are farmers who still prefer the companionship of a work animal to the impersonality of a tractor.

Early settlers often came into the mountains as single families. Working together, family members built a home. Many small cabins may be seen along the Parkway, reminders of the self-reliance demanded of our forefathers.

western mountains remained mostly Indian territory, defended by the Cherokee until after the end of the Revolutionary War.

These first colonists, of German, English, and Scotch-Irish ancestry, came from Pennsylvania and the piedmont, or foothill region, of North Carolina seeking freedom and land of their own. They came in small groups or sometimes in single families. In the great wilderness they found a piece of land which looked good to them and marked it as their own. The hollows and coves which they found were usually not large enough to support many families, so the tendency was for most families to be isolated from their neighbors by the ridges and forest. Often their nearest neighbors were five miles away through the wilderness. In places there were 30 miles between families who did not know of each other's exis-

tence. Small groups of people might form a tiny community along a river or in a large valley, but these "towns" were few and far between.

Owing to the great difficulties of travel, these first residents did not bring much with them—a Bible, a few tools, and some seeds. The whole family set to work clearing the land, cutting trees for a cabin, and planting their first garden, which they jealously guarded from small animals. When fall came, they preserved all that they had harvested, drying fruit and vegetables and storing potatoes and apples against the long winter ahead. The men hunted—the women and children gathered berries and nuts. In addition, the women made clothes, blankets, and mattress ticking. Nearly everything had to be handmade—quilts, baskets, shoes, and even tools. They discovered which woods in the forest were good for making a spoon, or a chair, or a yoke for the oxen. As time went on, the new inhabitants learned, perhaps from the Indians, how to find wild plants to use for medicines. Certain individuals became known for their ways of healing, and they would be sent for by their neighbors in times of sickness and childbirth. The families grew, and as there were more children there was more help. In later years the colonists could clear a little more land and improve their cabin. It was an isolated life and the work was hard. People aged early, but they had their freedom, and the land they worked was their own.

As more pioneers came, they formed small settlements. Those who lived out in the wilderness made the journey to town two or three times a year to barter their apples, vegetables, corn liquor, or wild plants for supplies they needed—

DAVID CATLIN

Using available light, mountain women made quilts to keep their families warm. In the early days they also made clothes, sheets, and mattress ticking.

sugar, salt, soda, and coffee, or perhaps a new plow or a calf. When there were enough inhabitants in a community, they built churches which were often also used as schools. The term was short—two or three months out of the year. Only when they could be spared from work around the farm did the children attend school.

Although relatively isolated, news from other areas was brought in by people migrating in and out of the mountains, by miners challenging the Blue Ridge for the ore beneath the mountains, by loggers who came to harvest the forests, and by drovers leading their cattle to market.

Both subsistence farmers and yeomen farmers tilled the rocky and not always generous

JAMES PAGANO

In addition to its stock of goods for sale, the community's general store was the center of information. Here the residents received their mail and learned news from beyond the mountains.

13

In the days before modern insulation, mountain people often pasted newspapers on their cabin walls to keep the cold winter air from filtering in through the logs and chinking. These papers are a reminder of the days when mail order catalogs and newspaper advertisements were the stuff of which dreams were made:

Best dinnerware $6.98
Shoes $1.66 - $1.98
Muslin 9¢ - 11¢ per yard.

mountain soil. It was a way of life which formed certain qualities in these mountaineers. They were independent, believing in their right to live life as they wanted and allowing others to do the same. They took care of their families and were hospitable to their neighbors. They believed in God and their own abilities.

The pace of their lives was governed by the changing seasons. They worked hard from spring until fall. When winter came and the demands of farming slowed, they could feel satisfied that they had accomplished much. They were not caught up in the frantic pace of the outside world trying to "get ahead" or following every "new-fangled" notion.

In dignified repose a small family graveyard blooms with the flowers of spring.

The timber industry and railroads brought major changes to the area during the late nineteenth century. By the 1930s, improved roads were built encouraging increasing numbers of people to come here to live. As the population grew, more towns were established and new ways of making a living surfaced. These innovations existed along with the old values—loyalty to one's family and neighbors, a love of freedom, and a belief in the right to be left alone.

There is a real feeling that today's mountaineers live side by side with their ancestors. Many residents still live on the original property settled by their forebears—some in the very same house, which has been modified to include all modern conveniences. Other descendants cherish their grandmother's churn or their grandfather's handmade bed. They can recall when their family first came to this ridge or that hollow, and they can tell innumerable stories of the life that was lived here.

The past endures on the Blue Ridge, visible in physical things such as old farm houses, cabins, and old tools, but more subtly viable in spiritual values and attitudes of the modern mountain people.

SUGGESTED READING

DYKEMAN, WILMA. *The Tall Woman.* New York: Holt, Rinehard, and Winston, 1962.

EHLE, JOHN. *The Landbreakers.* Evanston, Illinois: Harper and Row, 1964.

KEPHART, HORACE. *Our Southern Highlanders.* Macmillan Company, 1913. Reprinted, Knoxville: University of Tennessee Press, 1976.

The chill air of winter settles over the mountains, causing the pace of human activity to slow. Rime ice encases the limbs of trees.

DAVID CATLIN

15

The Building of the Parkway

Until the 1930s there were few roads in the remote rural sections of the mountains. Many of those which did exist were steep and rocky dirt tracks, usually crossing several streams which had to be forded. When the rains came, the thoroughfares became impassable mud bogs. Under these conditions, horses and wagons, oxcarts, and wooden sleds remained reliable means of transportation.

Even in its infancy, the automobile evoked visions of grandeur. There were those who foresaw that it would change the world. One of these men was Colonel Joseph Hyde Pratt, head of the North Carolina Geological Survey. As early as 1909 Pratt had envisioned a recreational road on top of the mountains. He called it the "Crest of the Blue Ridge Highway." He even managed to have a short section of it built in the vicinity of Altapass, North Carolina, but World War I halted the project. To become a reality, the recreational motor road had to wait for the Great Depression.

By 1933, President Franklin D. Roosevelt was authorizing funds for public works projects all

Along the corridor the natural beauty of the landscape predominates. The split rail fences of Appalachia often border the thoroughfare.

Immaculately maintained, the highway entices the motorist into the distant mountains.

Changing weather patterns are to be expected. A temporary blanket of fog lends mystery to the scene.

DAVID CATLIN

over the United States to relieve the economic depression. One type of project was the construction, repair, and improvement of public highways and parkways. When President Roosevelt visited the first Civilian Conservation Corps (CCC) camp in Virginia, he traveled over a portion of the Skyline Drive, which members of that camp had helped to build. It was suggested to the President that this road be extended, or that a similar route be constructed through the mountains, to connect the Shenandoah National Park to the Great Smoky Mountains National Park. Mr. Roosevelt approved of the suggestion.

For the next year many influential men in the East discussed the idea. One point of argument was the proposed route and how it would be shared by Virginia, North Carolina, and Tennessee. Selection of the route was of vital importance to the states involved, because they

Sunlight bathes high pastures near Doughton Park. Landscape architects and engineers carefully selected the location of the roadway for its diversity of scenery. America's longest national park, the Blue Ridge Parkway extends for 469 miles.

BILL BAKE

18

At higher altitudes the road winds through the Canadian forest zone. Visitor centers are located at intervals throughout the park.

thought that it would greatly speed economic recovery of the region through which it passed. The decision was up to Secretary of the Interior Harold Ickes, who finally chose the Virginia-North Carolina route.

The road was to be a joint project of the Commonwealth of Virginia, the United States government and the state of North Carolina. The federal government's share was assigned to the National Park Service, working in cooperation with the Bureau of Public Roads. The states were to obtain the right-of-way at their own expense, and the federal government would provide monies from public works funds for building the highway.

Survey parties were in the field by 1934, and construction began in September 1935. The Parkway was built in non-contiguous sections—one here, one there—until it was completed. The average width of right-of-way was set at 1,000 feet, with no portion to be less than 200 feet. An act of Congress on June 30, 1936, placed the Blue Ridge Parkway under the jurisdiction of the National Park Service.

Along its entire 469 miles, the Blue Ridge Parkway was skillfully planned by landscape architects of the National Park Service and engineers of the Bureau of Public Roads. The intent was to provide a great variety of visual experiences and, by the use of overlooks, to create the illusion that this was a park with boundaries extending to the horizon. In addition to the basic corridor, the design called for a series of recreation areas to be developed. Today there are 18 of these areas, varying in size from 250 acres to 6,000 acres.

SUGGESTED READING

JOLLEY, HARLEY E. *The Blue Ridge Parkway.* Knoxville: University of Tennessee Press, © 1969. Fourth printing, 1977.

A Journey Along the Parkway

It is the mandate of the Blue Ridge Parkway to conserve and interpret the unique natural and cultural resources of the southern Appalachian highlands. At the roadside overlooks and recreation areas there is an interweaving of natural history and human culture. The following are selections from among many attractions. Numbers in parentheses refer to milepost markers which have been placed at the side of the highway, beginning with "0" at the northern end.

Adjoining the Skyline Drive of the Shenandoah National Park, the Blue Ridge Parkway begins at Rockfish Gap with milepost 0. Tree-covered ridges are interspersed with overlooks of lovely valleys in Virginia.

ROCKFISH GAP TO ROANOKE (0 - 120)

The northern section of the Parkway, from Rockfish Gap to Roanoke, is called the Ridge Province. The road rises and falls in long graceful, curving slopes, passing through 105 miles of national forest. In the high forest the Parkway criss-crosses the famous Appalachian Trail, a hiker's footpath which follows the Appalachian Mountains for 2,050 miles from Maine to Georgia.

At intervals along the Parkway there are open vistas where one may gaze from the heights at the beautiful Shenandoah Valley and at the Allegheny Mountains beyond. At Otter Creek the Parkway reaches its lowest elevation at 649.4 feet.

In the following 15 miles the road rises 3,200 feet to Apple Orchard, highest point in Virginia, on the outskirts of the Peaks of Otter. From the Peaks, the road gracefully descends the ridge to the Roanoke Valley.

Rockfish Gap (0) It is appropriate that the trip on the Blue Ridge Parkway begins with a "gap." In the terminology of the mountain people, a gap is a low place in the mountains, a dip in the ridge (known as a "pass" or a "notch," in other parts of the country). These were the places where the mountains could be crossed most easily—Indians, settlers, and wild game all came through the gaps.

The Humpback Rocks form a sharp profile against the sky. This outcropping of greenstone is one of many unique rock formations to be encountered along the Parkway.

Humpback Rocks (5.8) The featured exhibit here is the pioneer farm. Perhaps no place on the Parkway offers the visitor such a graphic experience of what life must have been like for those first families who came alone into the mountain wilderness and made a home for themselves. The buildings consist of a cabin and small outbuildings. The earliest mountaineers made their homes from what was here—rocks and trees. Trees were felled and from them logs were cut and hand hewn. Ends of the logs were notched so that they would fit together. Once the logs were in place, the spaces in between were filled with mixtures of mud and lime called "chinking." Foundations and chimneys were made of rocks, abundant in the mountains.

It is a constant surprise to see the many uses to which mountain residents put the rocks and the beauty inherent in these structures. For many miles through woods on the Humpback Rocks there are stone fences. These were built to control the wanderings of half-wild hogs as they foraged for acorns and chestnuts. The hogs are gone, but the fences remain, silent and enduring testimony to the industry of those who made them.

The outbuildings of the mountain farm have a charm all their own. These buildings were constructed in the same way as the cabin, and each had its own special purpose. There were barns, smokehouses, corncribs, animal pens, and root cellars. In the cool darkness of the springhouse, water constantly flowed through a trough. Here the mountain woman placed jugs of milk, crocks of butter, and whatever else she wanted to keep cool. To walk among the outbuildings is to perceive the hard work and thriftiness of the mountaineer, the buildings themselves a reminder that life depended not just upon growing food, but also upon the ability to preserve and store it.

The center of activity was the mountain cabin. If the cabin door is open, it is easy to imagine that the family has just stepped outside. There is a fire burning in the stone fireplace, iron pots stand ready to be filled with tonight's dinner, and green beans from the garden are on the table waiting to be snapped. A bright quilt covers the bed, and on the quilting frame someone has left her needle and thread in place on the quilt in progress. In the loft above, children's shoes rest beside their pallets. On the front porch someone is

WALTER MCQUARRY

CONNIE TOOPS

Early settlers built their cabins and outbuildings from native materials—trees and rocks. The lower section of the root cellar provided a dark, cool place for storing vegetables. Logs were notched at the ends to provide a snug fit.

Overleaf:
"Tis distance lends enchantment to the view, And robes the mountain in its azure hue." —Thomas Campbell, 1777-1844. Photo by David Muench.

Map of Blue Ridge Parkway
The map starting on this page follows the full length of the Blue Ridge Parkway from north to south—from Virginia to North Carolina.

making a split-oak basket, and in the corner is a pile of soft newly shorn wool, ready to be spun. There is much to see and contemplate here about a way of life so different from our own.

Along the forested ridges south of Humpback, there are hickory and oak trees. Early settlers used the bark of the chestnut oak. In spring the bark was stripped from the trees and was used as a source of tannin for curing hides and making leather. In early times in the mountains there were craftsmen who made shoes for their neighbors. In later years the tanbark was sold for cash and shipped off to shoe manufacturers. Hickory nuts provided food for animals of the woods as well as for people, and hickory chips were used in curing hams.

COURTESY NATIONAL PARK SERVICE, PUBLICATIONS DIVISION

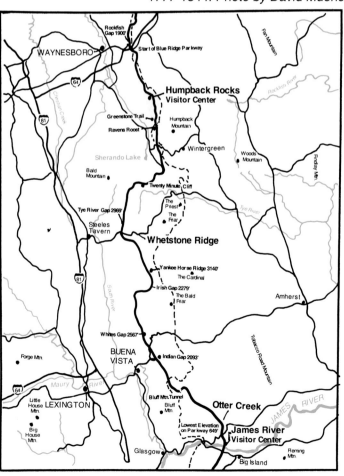

Brilliant autumn leaves float down a mountain stream, catching on stones. At Otter Creek the Parkway reaches its lowest elevation of 649.4 feet.

DAVID MUENCH

the heart of colonial Virginia. The river was an important transportation corridor. Mountain and piedmont farmers traveled the James in flatboats, taking their crops of tobacco and grain to market.

River travel was vastly improved at the suggestion, some say, of George Washington. In other locations in the country in the early 1800s, canals were proving useful as a means of transporting goods to market. Why not build a series of canals through the Blue Ridge, across the Alleghenies, to connect the James with the Ohio River system? For those who have traveled these ridges, it is hard to believe that anyone really thought that this was a feasible idea. It is even harder to believe that it was actually carried out—at least in part.

The James River and Kanawha Company built almost 200 miles of a canal system which ran westward from Richmond across the Blue Ridge

The land furnished the settlers with other necessities. For instance, Whetstone Ridge is reputedly named for a high quality of sandstone found there which made a good whetstone for sharpening blades. Beyond Whetstone Ridge, there is a walk in the forest which features a short section of track from a logging railroad used in the 1920s. The timber industry brought many changes to the mountains.

James River (63.7) Originating in the Alleghenies to the west, the James River cuts through the Blue Ridge and flows to the Atlantic Ocean through

Walking on the logging railroad at Yankee Horse Ridge. Most Appalachian mountain forests were logged during the early 1900s.

BILL BAKE

Flowing to the Atlantic Ocean, the James River was once an important transportation route from the mountains.

to Buchanan. The first link was operational by 1840, and the entire route to Buchanan was completed by 1851. The company might eventually have accomplished its plan of reaching the Ohio, but the introduction of railroads forecast the demise of canal systems.

During its heyday, however, the canal system was important to the development of the great valley, and during the Civil War it served the Confederacy as a means of transporting supplies. But by the 1880s, the canal was a thing of the past. Today, there is a lock on the James River restored as a Parkway exhibit. The visitor may stand at the lock, look up along the river and into the mountains, and marvel at the indomitable spirit of those who would get through these mountains, one way or another.

Crossing the James River, the traveler enters the Jefferson National Forest and makes the dramatic climb to the Peaks of Otter. The woods nearby enclose the road. Gazing into their density, one begins to comprehend how the great forests combined with the ridges to separate mountain communities. One needs to walk among these trees to appreciate how that enforced separation also created an identification with, and intense love of, the woods.

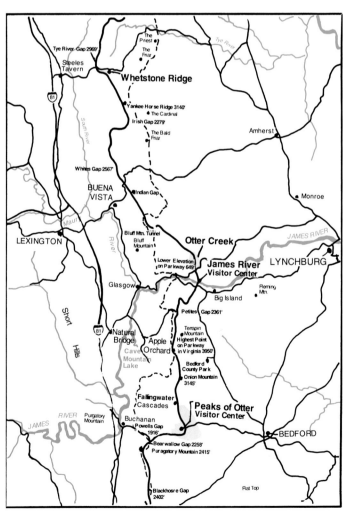

27

A curious raccoon seems somewhat surprised to be observed.

There are many woodland trails along the Parkway—they are all different and each offers a special experience. Sometimes the path follows along a mountain stream with rocks, waterfalls, and quiet pools. Many varieties of beautiful ferns, soft green mosses of different textures, and strange lichens flourish. Walking on beneath the trees, one notices the bark on the trunks—shiny yellow birch, which glistens gold in the muted light, the rich red of the cherry tree, or the blue-gray of ironwoods.

From spring to fall one hears the singing of tiny warblers or the drumming of woodpeckers on hollow trunks. Chipmunks streak across the path or make a racket in the leaves. In spring there is a profusion of wildflowers on the forest floor: jack-in-the-pulpit, white or deep red trillium, mayapple, violets, columbine, and wild iris.

The clarity of morning light enhances the beauty of the Peaks of Otter.

In summer there is shaded green light filtering through the canopy of leaves, and in fall there are extensive patches of brilliant red and gold—color above and color on the ground. In winter the forests are a study in contrast—black trunks against the snow.

For the people of the mountains, seasonal changes measure the passage of time in their lives. The early settlers lived in the woods and walked in them of necessity. The forest became a part of the very fabric of their lives. Although the uses of the forest's gifts are discussed in exhibits throughout the Parkway, to understand what the forest meant to the spirit of the southern highlander, one needs to walk these woodland paths.

Peaks of Otter (84) There are places in the world which just seem to invite people through an enchantment all their own. The Peaks of Otter is such a place. High in the Virginia mountains, a small valley nestles between two peaks called Sharp Top and Flat Top. Archaeological evidence indicates that prehistoric Indians camped here. At the time that explorers discovered the area, there were well-established Indian trails. Settlers later built a road here which was used as a supply route during the Revolutionary War. By about 1830 a small inn had been constructed and, by 1860, a resort hotel, the Mons.

The Johnson Farm, built about 1850, was in continual use until the 1920s. The National Park Service has restored this farm to its 1920 appearance. One may walk to the farm via a footpath and the remains of a wagon road. At the barn are examples of tools used during the Johnson Farm's early days.

For many years there was a community in the valley between the Peaks. Many of the residents who lived here earned their livelihood by working for and/or selling vegetables and other farm products to the Mons Hotel. The families continued many traditional customs. They would come together at one another's houses for wood choppings, corn huskings, bean shellings, and oat cuttings. The family at the Johnson Farm raised almost all the food they needed for themselves.

In communities like this one, young people made their own entertainment. At Christmas they had firecrackers, and in winter they went sledding. Often there was music and dancing at various homes. Like other mountaineers, they loved to tell stories. One account concerned an early-day escapade at the Peaks of Otter:

DAVID MUENCH

In October the colors of autumn adorn the ridges.

On the 4th of July, 1820, a group of local young men took on a challenge from the mountain. There was a large rock, about 20 or 30 feet high, which was balanced on the very top of Sharp Top. The young men decided that they would push this rock off of the peak. Gathering on the mountaintop, the men pushed and pried and shoved. They worked all day, but the rock would not budge. They tried using black powder, but to no avail. Finally, combining powder and wedges, they managed in a great effort to pry it loose, and it went crashing down the mountain, leveling huge trees and dislodging boulders until it came to rest in the woods below. In 1852, the people of Bedford, wishing to contribute something to the Washington Monument, then being built, blasted this rock and sent a large chunk to Washington, D.C.. Today, it rests in the west wall of the Monument, at the 12th stairway landing, bearing this inscription:

From Otter's summit,
Virginia's loftiest peak,
To crown a monument
To Virginia's noblest son.

Leaving the Peaks of Otter behind, the Parkway follows the ridge through the forest and gradually descends to the valley of the Roanoke River.

Farms Along the Parkway

For much of its length the Parkway corridor adjoins small, privately owned farms. Fields are planted with tobacco, hay, corn, cabbage, and beans. Neighboring farmers sometimes lease Parkway land for raising crops or pasturing livestock. In many cases, the farmers are descendants of original settlers of the area. Today, although pickup trucks and tractors have largely replaced wagons and horse-drawn plows, evidence remains of the old ways. Here and there a rusted hayrake in the farmyard, or plows converted to mail-box posts suggest another time and another way of living.

DAVID CATLIN

CONNIE TOOPS

The Johnson Farm, located at the Peaks of Otter, has been restored to resemble its appearance in the 1920s. Reached via a footpath and wagon road, the exhibit includes the house, outbuildings, and tools.

Relics of a bygone era, old farm implements such as this hayrake may still be seen on farms along the road.

THE HIGHLAND PLATEAU: ROANOKE TO BLOWING ROCK (120-290)

From Roanoke south to the vicinity of Blowing Rock, North Carolina, the Parkway traverses the Blue Ridge Plateau. To the east the Blue Ridge drops dramatically to the piedmont below. Distant vistas alternate with nearby highland farms. From Roanoke south, the Blue Ridge is also the divide between the drainages to the Atlantic Ocean and the Gulf of Mexico. West of the ridge the waters find their way through mountain valleys to the Gulf; eastward, the waters cascade down steep mountainsides to the piedmont and on to the Atlantic.

Entering the plateau country, the Parkway meanders through scenes of quiet rural beauty, the landscape gently shaped by generations of residents. On small farms that border the road, farmers cultivate the ground adjacent to the Parkway along with the rest of their land, pasturing cattle and horses, or planting row crops of

DAVID CATLIN

DAVID CATLIN

Its days of bustling activity past, the Johnson Farm is now serene.

corn, beans, cabbage, or tobacco. In order to preserve these rural landscapes, the Parkway administration works with neighboring farmers in a variety of ways. Parkway land has often been purchased outright, and then contracted by agricultural lease. Or, the property may be under a "scenic easement" regulation, by which it belongs to the farmer, but he agrees to use it in ways compatible with the visual objectives of the park. It is one of the unique features of this park that it has 4,000 to 5,000 private landowners bordering the thoroughfare, yet it still maintains the feeling of a great, wide national park.

On these mountain farms are tangible mixtures of old and new—the ancient barn next to the modern farmhouse; the shiny new pickup truck parked beside the horse-drawn cultivator. Changes go beyond the farm. Retail sales and factory work, fast food and contemporary fashions are all part of mountain life today.

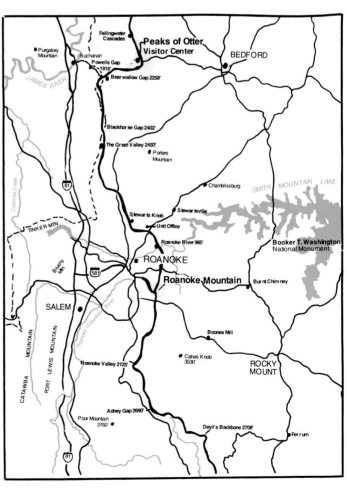

Lovely beds of ferns are frequently encountered in the forest.

Crested dwarf iris.

WALTER MCQUARRY

Trout lilies catching the sunlight.

M. WOODBRIDGE WILLIAMS

Smart View (154.5) In spring, when dogwood trees at Smart View are draped in the delicate lace of their blossoms, local people gather for an enduring custom of the mountains—the family reunion. In small towns where one or two original families had many children, these reunions of their descendants may involve practically the whole community. When they get together once a year, picnic tables are covered with tablecloths and buried beneath home-cooked dishes made from recipes handed down through generations— apple butter, homemade pickles, green beans, corn bread, country ham, and blueberry pie. "Claiming kin" is a means of verifying one's identity. In the practice of this tradition, modern mountain residents reaffirm their sense of belonging. The community gains strength by acknowledging that its roots are long, its branchings many.

Rocky Knob (167) From the gentle pastureland of Smart View the highway climbs the slopes to Rocky Knob. From here one looks down Rock Castle Gorge. Named for the crystalline quartz particles found in the area, the gorge was farmed until 1935, and one may still see the remains of steep hillside farms. There are ways to recognize the site of a former homestead on land along the Parkway. Here and there an old rock chimney stands alone in a field, or on a hill lies a small cemetery. In these family graveyards the head-stones were often chiseled by hand. There are always baby graves, for mountain families had many children, and the toll exacted by childhood sickness and disease was great.

Along with these man-made signs of previous occupancy, there are natural ones as well. Frequently encountered are small apple orchards, their ancient trees now gnarled and twisted, gray-green with moss. Sometimes one comes upon a lilac, now grown into a "thickety bush," a reminder of a woman of long ago who planted this bit of color and fragrance near her door.

Woodland trails starting from many overlooks invite the visitor to enjoy a quiet interlude in the forest or to set out on an all-day hike.

M. WOODBRIDGE WILLIAMS

Devil's Bit, also called Blazing Star or Fairy Wand.

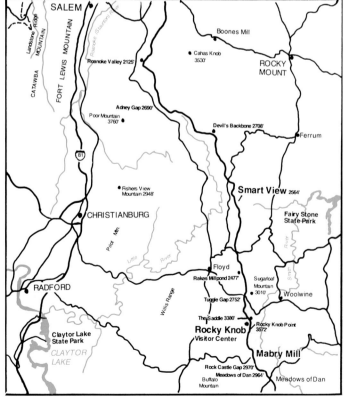

Mabry Mill (176) The exhibit at Mabry Mill is a monument to the diversity of one man's talents as well as a reminder of the ingenuity evolved by those who lived away from cities. Ed Mabry had learned to be a blacksmith. This trade was one of the most important in mountain communities. The blacksmith made an amazing variety of useful metal items, from door hinges to wagon parts to cooking implements. Having set up his blacksmith shop, Mabry went on to build a gristmill with its great waterwheel. He then used the power for grinding corn and for running a sawmill.

In the old days, when travel was difficult and towns were far away, people learned to make the things they needed. Most of them farmed, but they also developed the necessary skills of carpentry or leather tanning or blacksmithing. When someone in the area was particularly adept at one of these trades, he acquired a reputation, and people would come to him for assistance. Ed Mabry was a good example of this, but he was not unique. In most mountain villages if you "ask around," you will learn of an old-timer who was known for his versatility and ability to "fix things." For those of us who go to the store to buy shoes or who have no idea how a frying pan is made, the exhibit at Mabry Mill is a lesson in the value of possessing a variety of skills.

There is another interesting contrast to modern society here. We live in an age of "planned ob-

Perhaps the best loved of all attractions on the Parkway, Mabry Mill was important in the lives of nearby mountain families. Farmers brought their corn to be ground into meal at the gristmill, leaving a portion of the meal as payment for this service. The power from the waterwheel also ran a sawmill. Located nearby was the blacksmith shop built by Ed Mabry in 1910 and operated until 1935. The mill today is the central attraction of a National Park Service exhibit illustrating mountain industry.

ED COOPER

JACK JEFFERS

During the summer months visitors may watch a blacksmith at work, skillfully turning metal into useful items.

WILLIAM A. BAKE

The millkeeper provided an essential service to the mountain community.

Occasionally on fall weekends, visitors may enjoy the opportunity to see how things were done in the old days. The horse provides power for the grinding of sorghum to be made into molasses. The fragrance of apple butter slowly cooking over an open fire permeates the atmosphere.

solescence." When something breaks, we throw it away and buy a new one. In the mountains, people could not buy a new one; they learned to use and reuse everything. For example, flour and feed came in cloth sacks. The women used the material from these sacks for quilt pieces, quilt backing, aprons, and oftentimes for children's clothes. Metal was difficult to obtain, so the men saved old pieces of scrap metal. "You'd best keep it, one day you might find a use for it."

This habit, arising out of need, still prevails among modern mountaineers. Many of them have an abhorrence of throwing anything away, because one day they might find a use for it. As commerce in the mountains grew, individuals were accused of "hanging on to old junk." Today we extol the virtues of recycling. In doing so we are only adopting an old mountain tradition.

Down the road from Mabry Mill, near the Virginia-North Carolina state line, is the town of Galax. This town is named for one of the most cherished of all mountain plants. Growing in beds beneath tall trees, galax leaves are shaped like rounded, ruffled hearts with a shiny leathery texture, and are deep green or red in color. When winter comes and all seems bare and brown, the galax adds its lovely color to the forest floor.

These plants have played an important part in the lives of many mountain dwellers, as they were one of the "cash crops." In fall many families would go into the woods and gather galax leaves in burlap sacks. These gatherings could be sold to a local merchant, who would in turn ship them to florists all over the country. Galax leaves retain their vibrancy for a long time after being picked. In the days before refrigeration florists would use them in funeral wreaths and floral displays—a lasting bit of green to grace a winter grave. While not so common as it once was, the practice of gathering galax in the fall still exists in the mountains of North Carolina.

Cumberland Knob (217) This was the first recreation area to be opened on the Parkway. It is a favorite spot for the local people, who use it just like a city park, coming out on weekends to pitch horseshoes, play baseball, and have a family picnic. In this area the roadsides are thick with white pines. These trees grow quickly and to great heights. For these reasons, they have been planted in stands throughout the mountains to be harvested and sold for lumber.

BILL BAKE

A lovely groundcover, galax was often collected and sold to floral companies, providing income for mountain families.

Doughton Park (238) Formerly known as the Bluffs, this is an area of high, open meadowlands. Because there are gamelands below the mountaintops, there are many white-tailed deer in this area which come up in the evenings to feed on the pastures at Doughton Park.

Brinegar Cabin was the home of a weaver. It stands as a reminder of the importance of handcrafts to the early residents. Recent revival of the American handcraft industry has been a blessing for many mountain families. Not only has it brought income to these people, it has also encouraged them to remember or learn anew those crafts handed down in their families. The oldtimers made them of necessity—pieced quilts, bedspreads, chairs, baskets, and woven cloth.

These skills were also an outlet for artistic expression. In each item there is great beauty and individuality. The names of quilt patterns are charming: "Log Cabin," "Maple Leaf," "Bear Paw," "Rocky Road to California," "Texas Star," "Double Irish Chain," "Rose of Sharon," and "Double Wedding Ring." There are now craft guilds which provide markets for the work of the mountain people. The Parkway offers several locations where the visitor may admire or purchase these items.

From the lovely high meadows of Doughton one can see the changing terrain which will dominate the rest of the Parkway to the south—a great jumble of mountains. No longer in nice parallel ridges, the mountains of western North Carolina radiate in all directions. From here to the horizon are wave upon wave of blue mountains. In the late evening light, the most distant ridges seem to blend in with, and become part of, the sky itself.

There are small animals here—red and gray foxes, raccoons, bobcats, skunks, and opossums. Most of these animals travel up the ridges and down into the hollows at night. Often they can be seen crossing the Parkway. The early mountain pioneers hunted these animals for their fur or as food. Those hunting foxes and raccoons used dogs. For the foxhunter, a large part of this activity involved sitting on some hillside around a fire, listening to the barking of the dogs as they ran the foxes in the valleys below. Many mountain men still keep foxhounds or "coon dogs," and will spend hours telling of the great feats accomplished by their favorite animal. The old-timers ate raccoons and 'possums—the latter usually cooked with sweet potatoes.

LEONARD LEE RUE III / ANIMALS ANIMALS

A male indigo bunting.

Brinegar Cabin, home of a mountain weaver.

DAVID MUENCH

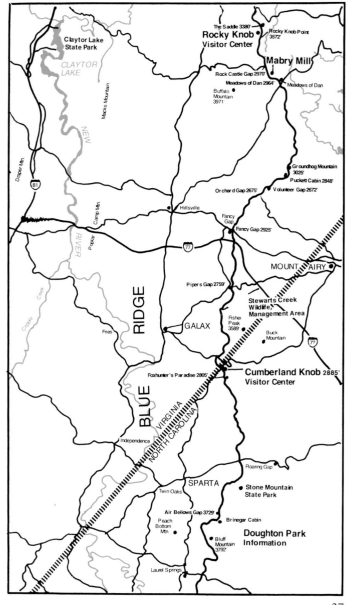

Another small animal which appears frequently along the roadside is the groundhog. It was also eaten by early mountaineers, and its hide was used for patch leather and shoelaces. Many an early homemade banjo had groundhog hide for the "head." The groundhog is celebrated in mountain song, and the sounds of the foxhounds and coon dogs find their way into dance tunes of the mountain fiddler and banjo player.

Weaving its way through the countryside south of Doughton, the Parkway passes several reconstructed cabins and an old church shelter (272). Pioneers often arrived in the mountains with a cherished family Bible. They took seriously both their work and their religion. When there were enough inhabitants in a community, they built churches. For those who lived up in the distant coves of the mountains, however, church services had to await the arrival of the circuit riders. These traveling preachers came in the spring as soon as the roads were passable, and their visits were greatly appreciated. When they came, they held services wherever there was room—in homes or outdoors. Sometimes a sort of rough shelter was constructed for this purpose.

The preacher had much to do during his stay. He conducted funeral services for those who had passed away during the winter, baptized babies and adults, and married young couples. Often the services continued for days. It was also a social occasion—a time to learn the news from the other side of the ridge, to see the new baby, and to become reacquainted with one's neighbors from the surrounding hills. And it was just good to be outside, now that winter was "lettin' up."

Dropping down the ridge to Deep Gap (276), the Parkway enters Daniel Boone country. In the mid-1700s this area of North Carolina was a wild and rugged wilderness known only to the passing Cherokee and the buffalo. At this time Daniel Boone was living below the mountains on the Yadkin River. He and other long hunters would take their muzzle-loading rifles into the mountains to hunt, often staying for months at a time.

When residents on the eastern seaboard first heard of the beautiful lands of Kentucky, the only route was to the north, through Virginia and across the great valley. The mountains of North Carolina were considered impassable. Boone was commissioned to cut a road through this wilderness. Following the old buffalo and Indian trails, he and a few companions carved a way later known as Boone's Trace. Daniel Boone eventually moved on to Kentucky to live, but his name re-

Appalachian dulcimer.

mains on local North Carolina features. He was one of the first explorers to travel in the wilderness, and his road was instrumental in opening up the "West."

Moses Cone Memorial Park (293) In North Carolina there is a long-standing tradition of mountain resort communities. The towns of Asheville, Linville, and Blowing Rock were, and still are, a part of this tradition. By the 1890s, visitors were coming to these areas to escape the heat of the piedmont and the coastal areas of the South. There were large hotels, and wealthy industrialists began to build summer homes where they might come to rest and escape the pressures of their work. One of these men was Moses H. Cone, a textile magnate known as "the Denim King." About 1895, near the town of Blowing

From dance tunes to ballads, mountain music may be heard at fiddlers' conventions throughout southern Appalachia.

Flat Top Manor, previous summer residence of the Moses Cone family, was built at the turn of the century. This 3,600-acre estate is now a recreation area featuring a craft center and 25 miles of winding carriage roads. On the front porch of the manor house, craftspeople demonstrate their skills.

Rock, North Carolina, Moses and Bertha Cone purchased 3,600 acres for their estate. Materials for their 20-room mansion had to be hauled up the mountain by oxcart.

When finished, the Cone estate was a fairly self-sufficient enterprise which contained its own dairy and flower and vegetable gardens. A carbide gas plant provided lighting for the house. The Cones employed local people, many of whom lived in small houses on the property. Moses Cone's personal hobby was road-building—on his estate he built 25 miles of beautiful carriage roads with smooth dirt surfaces. He also enjoyed cultivating apple trees. The estate produced 25 varieties of apples which ripened at various times from early spring to fall. Old-timers can recite the names of these apples, and tell which were for cooking, which were "keepers," and which were best for cider.

Mrs. Cone survived her husband by 39 years. Not long after her death in 1947, the estate became a part of the Parkway, to serve as a "public pleasure ground" and a memorial to Mr. Cone. The mansion now houses a craft shop, and the carriage roads offer visitors many miles of de-

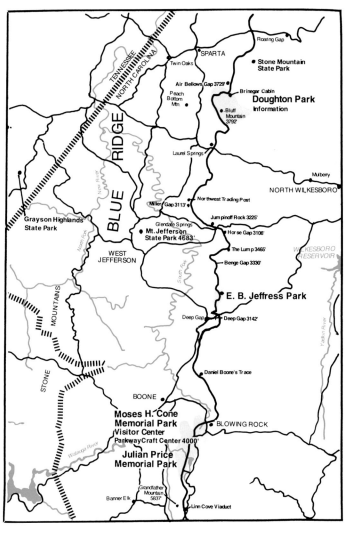

DAVID MUENCH

lightful rambling through the woods, around the pastures, and along the two small lakes.

Grandfather Mountain (300-306) Grandfather Mountain is one of the oldest mountains in the world and is the highest mountain in the Blue Ridge range. The rocks here are quartzite, one of the most durable of rock types. The roadway enters a densely forested area with a luxuriance of plant life under the trees. Farther into the forest the light is softer, more muted, and the surrounding world is made up of every imaginable shade of green. From the pale fronds of new ferns to the deep blue-green of hemlocks, each leaf reflects its light like the facets of an emerald. A closer examination of the ground reveals an astonishing variety of small plants—grasses and flowers, mosses and ferns.

In the late eighteenth and mid-nineteenth centuries two famous botanists, Andre Michaux and Asa Gray, visited the area. Both men were amazed at the abundant varieties of plants. They learned what mountain women had long known—that in the green forest there were gifts for those who knew how to find and use them. Many a mountain woman knew the uses of wild herbs for ministering to the needs of her family and her neighbors in times of illness. She also knew what time of year to enter the woods to gather these plants. Like the galax, medicinal plants could also be sold to local merchants. These "root and herb men" would then send them to pharmaceutical companies for use in medicines.

There are many caves and hiding places on the Grandfather. During the Civil War, deserters from both sides hid out here. Other occupants of the nearby hollows and coves and dark recesses were bears. Perhaps an old-timer will tell a lucky visitor a good bear yarn from earlier times on Grandfather Mountain.

Linn Cove (305) From quiet musings on the past, the traveler is suddenly awakened to the future. High on the slopes of the ancient mountain rises a wonder of modern technology. Seen from a distance, the Linn Cove Viaduct seems to flow out of the forest and float across the great boulders of

In a setting of virgin hemlock forest, the Linville River swirls and plunges over massive cliffs at Linville Falls.

Linn Cove Viaduct on Grandfather Mountain. At its completion in 1983, it was considered the most complicated concrete segmental bridge ever constructed.

HUGH MORTON

Linn Cove. This graceful structure was the solution to a complex engineering problem.

Linn Cove is a rugged and treacherous area of the mountain covered with massive rocks. Traditional road-building techniques would have required blasting the area, resulting in severe environmental damage. New methods of construction were required to protect the fragile landscape. The solution was to build an elevated roadway, or viaduct, designed specifically to fit the contours of the mountain.

Known as precast concrete segmental construction, the technique allowed the bridge to be built from the top down. The 153 precast segments of the bridge were formed separately at the site; they were then gradually joined. The only areas of the ground to be disturbed were at the base of each of the seven pillars that support the bridge.

Since its completion the viaduct has repeatedly won awards for engineering and design. Visitors come from afar to see it. As the culmination of 52 years of Parkway construction, the viaduct was the chosen site for the "grand opening" ceremony signaling completion of the Blue Ridge Parkway in 1987. This stunningly modern bridge graces the slopes of the venerable Grandfather Mountain. A nearby visitor center is open from May through October.

Lost Cove Overlook (310) While geologists are attracted to this area by the ancient rock formations, of more interest to local folks is the mystery of the Brown Mountain Lights. On many evenings out in the distant darkness above the shadowy hills, pale orange lights seem to appear, move around, then fade. No one seems able to explain what they are or why they are there, but there is much speculation on the subject. Stories about the Brown Mountain Lights form a chapter in the songs and folklore of this region.

Linville Falls (316) William Linville, a long hunter and contemporary of Daniel Boone, was killed by Indians in this vicinity. The river which bears his name winds through the forest, and then, makes a dramatic drop over rock ledges. Below the falls the river forms the bottom of Linville Gorge, now a wilderness area under the jurisdiction of the U.S. Forest Service.

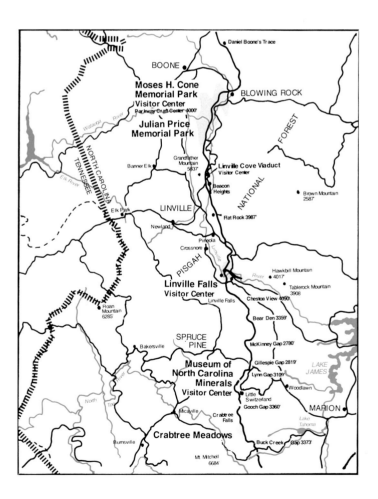

Trees of the Canadian forest zone are found on many high peaks of the southern section of the Parkway, beginning at Grandfather Mountain. Red spruce and Fraser fir are called "balsams" by local people. The dark color of these trees on the slopes gives the Black Mountains their name.

TOM ALGIRE

The trail to the falls is one of the few remaining places in the East where one may see the forest as it once was, for here a virgin stand of eastern hemlocks intermingles with white pines dating back 150 years. In the days when these mountains were heavily logged, areas of difficult access were left alone. When in later years loggers returned with better equipment, this stand was protected by its owners, who wanted the forest to remain untouched. It was then purchased by John D. Rockefeller Jr., and given to the National Park Service.

Many of the residents along this section of the Parkway make their living by raising Christmas trees and growing shrubbery—mountain laurel, rhododendron, azaleas, and blueberries. In winter a number of people add to their income by gathering club mosses and ground pines. These, along with pine branches, are woven into Christmas wreaths and evergreen decorations and are shipped to locations throughout the country.

South of Linville Falls the Parkway enters the mining district of the Spruce Pine region. The pegmatite intrusion which occurs here comprises one of the most highly mineralized areas in the world. The mines produce feldspar, kaolin, quartz, and mica. In the days before synthetics, the mica mines contributed to the production of

thin transparent sheets of isinglass and electrical insulating materials. In the eighteenth century Englishman Josiah Wedgewood made a journey here to obtain materials for his famous china. More recently, a pure grade of quartz from this area was used for the lens in the Mount Palomar telescope in California. Treasures from these hills have indeed found their way to distant places.

A marker at the Museum of North Carolina Minerals (331) commemorates the passage of the "overmountain men." In the days of the American Revolution, 1,000 backwoodsmen ceased fighting Indians just long enough to march down the mountains to the aid of beleaguered patriots. The march took them two weeks, and they carried their own rifles and supplies. They were called the overmountain men or the "backwater men" by those who lived farther east because they resided on the other side of the mountains, across the continental divide, where the waters flowed "backwards" to the Mississippi rather than "forwards" to the Atlantic. Their victory at the Battle of King's Mountain in South Carolina is said to have changed the course of the American Revolution.

Leaving the mining district, the road passes through beautiful forests with the Black Mountains looming darkly on the horizon. Beyond Crabtree Meadows (339) the Parkway be-

gins its last climb on the Blue Ridge. The vegetation changes; the southern forest intermingles with trees of the Canadian forest type—spruces and the black-green Fraser fir, which mountain people call balsam. At milepost 354, the Parkway takes leave of the Blue Ridge and skirts the southern edge of the Black Mountains. Shortly thereafter the highway enters the Great Craggy Mountains.

Leaving the Blue Ridge, the Parkway also exits the Atlantic-Gulf drainage divide. From here to the Great Smoky Mountains, the waters of the Parkway all flow toward the Gulf of Mexico. At this intersection of the three mountain ranges stands the highest mountain east of the Mississippi, Mount Mitchell, at 6,684 feet. A spur road from the Parkway leads to Mount Mitchell State Park at the summit.

Traversing the Great Craggies, one truly feels on top of the world. There are spectacular panora-

At Crabtree Meadows, a wooded trail leads down to Crabtree Falls, formed as the creek dances and froths and glimmers over the rocks. In spring wildflowers abound on the trail, and warblers, more often heard than seen, join their voices to the music of the falls.

mas of the mountains of western North Carolina on one side of the road, while on the other there are rugged rock cliffs. These rocks are usually dripping with water, their wet surfaces shining in the sunlight. All through the spring and summer there are delicate wildflowers in little clumps among the rocks—small bright bouquets of blue, yellow, and red. Sometimes clouds race across this high ridge and envelop it in fog which closes out the vast distances, causing one to focus on the immediate—the textures of nearby rocks; the dark balsam trees, stark against the white mist; and the awesome silence of this high mountain land. It is a place of changing weather, cool on the heights when it is warm in the valleys below. In fall one

may be surprised to reach these altitudes and find limbs of windswept, twisted trees encased in ice.

Craggy Gardens (363) The "Gardens" are named for the beds of Catawba rhododendron which cover the area. This is an example of a heath "bald." Areas such as this appear throughout the southern Appalachians. Seen from a distance, they give the appearance of "bald" spots among the forested heights. Balds are usually covered by grasses or mountain shrubbery of the heath family, such as rhododendron, mountain laurel, azaleas, and blueberries.

There are conflicting theories as to why balds occur. They may have been areas burned off by Indians to attract game or by early settlers to create grazing land for sheep and cattle. In spring Craggy Gardens are ablaze with the color of the Catawba rhododendron in bloom. While the Rosebay rhododendron prefers the cool shade of the forest, the Catawba enjoys open sunlight. When the gardens are in bloom there is a tropical profusion of red to purple blossoms.

From the heights of the Craggies the Parkway begins its gradual descent into the valley of the French Broad River, home of the city of

A petal-showered trail leads into the "gardens" of rhododendron atop the Great Craggy Mountains.

Visitors and local people alike make pilgrimages to see the Catawba rhododendron in bloom.

Open year-round, the Folk Art Center near Asheville, North Carolina, a Parkway visitor center, features sales and demonstrations of traditional and modern handcrafts.

NPS PHOTO

Asheville. The Folk Art Center (382) features sales and demonstrations of regional and contemporary crafts.

Passing the river valley, the road begins a steep climb through the Pisgah National Forest, leaving behind Asheville and seemingly all traces of modern civilization. Much of this land belonged to George W. Vanderbilt, who built a country estate, Biltmore, near Asheville in 1895. Vanderbilt purchased 130,000 acres of mountains and valleys and brought Dr. Carl Schenck here from Germany to begin the first forestry school in America. Young men from the mountains were brought here to live and to learn improved meth-

At the Cradle of Forestry one may learn the history of the first forestry school in America, now operated by the U.S. Forest Service.

BILL BAKE

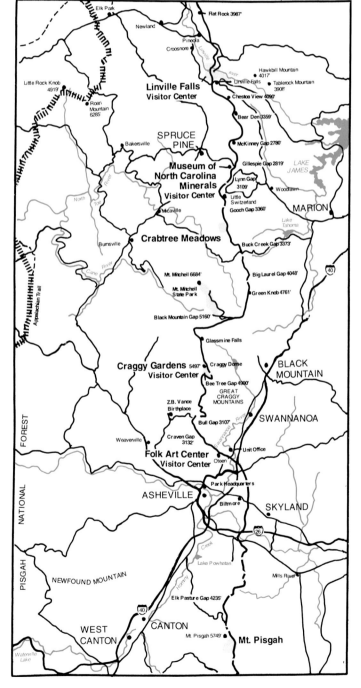

ods of forest management. At the Cradle of Forestry, just below the Parkway on Highway 276, the U.S. Forest Service operates an outdoor historic exhibit which tells about this early effort in forest management.

Mount Pisgah (408) The recreation area at Pisgah is the one area on the Parkway which is frequently visited by the black bear, and travelers are warned to watch for them. Lands below the Parkway along its entire length contain areas which are bear habitats, but Pisgah seems to be the only place at present where bears enter the campground. They are wild animals—one should keep a distance and feel fortunate to see them.

THE PISGAH LEDGE: MOUNT PISGAH TO THE GREAT SMOKY MOUNTAINS (408-469)

"Wild" is probably the best term to apply to this last section of the Parkway. The highway tra-

PAT TOOPS

The black bear, a seldom-seen resident of the forest.

verses the Pisgah, Balsam, and Plott Balsam ranges before terminating at the foot of the Great Smoky Mountains. High on the Pisgah Ledge, the terrain is composed of rocky cliff faces and views of tier after tier of distant mountains. One moment the road sweeps to the edges of the cliffs, the next it plunges back into the dense forest.

Here was the home of wild animals, a fact reflected in the many overlooks which are named for bears and bear hunters. The bears are still here, although many of the other wild creatures no longer dwell in these woods. Elk and buffalo were gone by 1800—beaver had disappeared by 1900. Until about 1920 there were wolves in the mountains. The mountain lion, called a panther, or "painter" by mountain people, is thought to have disappeared by 1920. However, rumors persist that some of these magnificent cats have survived and still live in the wild places. They certainly live on in stories of the mountain folk. A visitor on this southern end of the Parkway finds it easy to imagine the big cats stealthily roaming the dark woods and rocky cliffs of the Pisgah and Balsam ranges.

Though elk and buffalo no longer migrate across the ridges, there are other migrants on the Pisgah Ledge. In fall monarch butterflies cross by the hundreds, fluttering toward the South and Mexico. Hawks, too, may be seen migrating in fall. The Appalachians are a flyway, and spring and fall provide excellent bird-watching seasons along the entire Parkway. The traveler who is particularly

DAVID MUENCH

In earlier times the mountain ranges of western North Carolina were the home of the Great Cherokee Nation, and the habitat of bears, wolves, and mountain lions.

alert may see ruffed grouse or wild turkeys along roadsides in the Pisgahs and Balsams.

Richland Balsam (431) At this point the Parkway reaches its highest elevation—6,053 feet. The overlooks open on distant panoramas of the myriad ranges of the southern Appalachians: the Cowees, Nantahalas, and Plott Balsams. The habitat of wild animals, these ranges were also the home of the great Cherokee Nation, its villages located along the streams, it trails crossing the ridges and gaps. In the names of geographical features in this area we are reminded of those first encounters between Indians and pioneers. For its last ten miles, the Parkway passes through the Cherokee Indian Reservation. In the town of Cherokee, at the foot of the Great Smoky Mountains, the Cherokee tell their own story in the Museum of the Cherokee, an outdoor drama, and a Living Indian Village. This was their land first—their story is worth knowing.

In towns throughout the mountains, residents still enjoy community get-togethers. They are particularly fond of celebrations of all sorts—apple festivals, craft fairs, clogging contests, fiddlers' conventions—even an observance revolving around the ramp, or wild onion. Mountaineers have a keen sense of fun, and at these events they dance, sing, and joke with one another.

Central to all these events is the music. The strong musical tradition of the mountains can be traced back to the days when ballads and dance tunes were passed around from person to person along with the stories. Listening to the music, one is struck by how many of the songs tell of home in the mountains.

Though the people of Appalachia may leave to serve in the military or to seek employment elsewhere, the mountains are always home. Many who go away in younger years will return later in life. Those who never come back here to live retain their psychological ties with their home place. Some individuals never leave at all. Of the values which have endured here, these are the strongest—the mountain dwellers' love of their homeland and their sense of identity with these mountains.

SUGGESTED READING

LORD, WILLIAM G. *Blue Ridge Parkway Guide.* Asheville, North Carolina: Hexagon Company, 1976.

PEATTIE, RODERICK, ED. *The Great Smokies and the Blue Ridge: The Story of the Southern Appalachians.* New York: The Vanguard Press, 1943.

ED BOWER

High on the Pisgah Ledge, vast distances stretch out before one's gaze. Looking Glass Rock receives its name from the light reflected from its surface when wet.

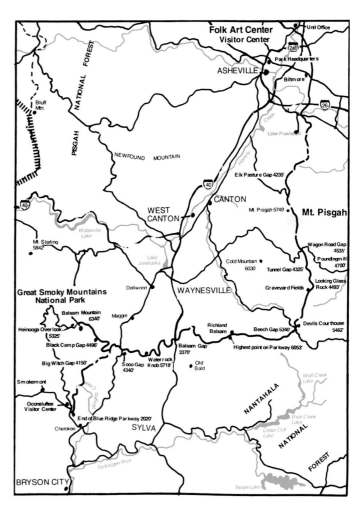

WILLIAM A. BAKE

Blue Ridge Parkway Today

The spirit of the Blue Ridge Parkway is embodied in its variety—mountains, forests, wildlife, and the people of the southern highlands. While one may take home photographs and mental images of the scenic wonders, the influence of mountain culture is more subtle. The crafts, the songs, the way of life with its slower pace and its values of family closeness, kindness to one's neighbors, and strong sense of community—these are impressions to be contemplated long after one leaves.

The Blue Ridge Parkway is inextricably bound to the neighbors on its fringes. As communities along the corridor change, so must the visual impact of the road itself change. While seemingly so indomitable, the mountains are not immune to destruction—modern man has learned to move mountains. With care and understanding this landscape can be preserved, so that future visitors may travel the Blue Ridge Parkway and experience the uplifting of the human spirit which comes to those who journey through the southern highlands.

Inside back cover: Natives of the mountains—fragile blossoms, evergreen leaves, enduring rock. Photo by David Muench.

Back cover: Near the Virginia-North Carolina state line, Mabry Mill tells a story of the mountain way of life. Photo by M. Woodbridge Williams.

KC Publications has been the leading publisher of colorful, interpretive books about National Park areas, public lands, Indian lands, and related subjects for over 40 years. We have 6 active series—over 135 titles—with Translation Packages in up to 8 languages for over half the areas we cover. Write, call, or visit our web site for our full-color catalog.

Our series are:

The Story Behind the Scenery® – Compelling stories of over 65 National Park areas and similar Public Land areas. Some with Translation Packages.

in pictures... The Continuing Story® – A companion, pictorially oriented, series on America's National Parks. All titles have Translation Packages.

For Young Adventurers™ – Dedicated to young seekers and keepers of all things wild and sacred. Explore America's Heritage from A to Z.

Voyage of Discovery® – Exploration of the expansion of the western United States.

Indian Culture and the Southwest – All about Native Americans, past and present.

Calendars – For National Parks in dramatic full color, and a companion Color Your Own series, with crayons.

To receive our full-color catalog featuring over 135 titles—Books, Calendars, Screen Scenes, Videos, Audio Tapes, and other related specialty products:

Call (800-626-9673), fax (702-433-3420), write to the address below, Or visit our web site at www.kcpublications.com

Published by KC Publications, 3245 E. Patrick Ln., Suite A, Las Vegas, NV 89120.

Created, Designed, and Published in the U.S.A.
Printed by Tien Wah Press (Pte.) Ltd, Singapore
Pre-Press by United Graphic Pte. Ltd